ALL
THE
MONEY
YOU
NEED

George L. Ford

WORD BOOKS, PUBLISHER
WACO, TEXAS

To those who
struggle with financial problems
and long to be free

CONTENTS

PREFACE

If you want to know how to become a millionaire, you've got the wrong book. But if you want to know how to get out of debt, pay your bills on time, and raise your standard of living on your present income, read on.

I had gotten somewhat of a reputation for helping Christian organizations get out of debt. I was able to establish controls and build fund-raising programs. But I hadn't really taken the time to watch-dog my own personal financial affairs. We never got in as deep as many do. We lived within our income, paid our bills. Our two children graduated from a Christian high school and Christian colleges. We had a retirement program and some insurance. But we sometimes got trapped in the tempting revolving charge account bit. I'm afraid we really didn't know how much money it gobbled up.

My work for twenty years kept me on the road, away from home many lonely hours, days, and weeks. To make up for this I took the family with me whenever possible. We had wonderful times together, crisscrossing our country, into Canada, and dipping south of the border into Mexico. We all enjoyed life, but it took a lot of money.

Then five years ago, soon after my fifty-sixth birthday, our rainy day hit with a crashing thunderstorm. "Brain tumor," the doctor said. The tests seemed endless; then surgery. Convalescence was slow. Agonizing questions tumbled on us day after day. Disability? Would I ever work again? What kind of job could I get? Near panic.

In the midst of our darkest days God gave us this verse:

"You shall eat the fruit of the labor of your hands; you shall be happy, and it shall be well with you" (Ps. 128:2).

In answer to our prayers and the prayers of many friends, God has restored me to a place of responsibility. And through this experience we've learned how to take better care of what God gives us. That's what I want to share with you.

The approach is practical. I've used some of our own experiences and those of some of the families I have counseled. The people are real, but their identity is camouflaged. You may think you see yourself in some of the stories for there are many similarities in family financial situations.

If this book helps you do a better job of taking care of what God gives you, I'll be thankful. And God will be pleased.

George L. Ford

CHAPTER 1

DO YOU HAVE FINANCIAL FREEDOM?

Bill and Mary knew they were in trouble. There was never enough money to go around. The rent came first; they couldn't skip that. The car payment could be delayed sometimes, but after two delinquent notices they had to take care of it. Now they had to pay it every month, but it was always at least a month behind.

It had been easy to buy new furniture when they moved to Springfield. They just signed the papers and agreed to pay "a little" each month. They had opened revolving charge accounts at two department stores; the interest was only 1.5

percent a month. They used credit cards for gas and other car expenses. They didn't have to pay all the bills every month, just a "minimum" amount. The rest only cost them the usual 1.5 percent a month interest. The two bank credit cards were easy to get and very handy. They could buy almost anything at almost any store and pay by the month, with just 1.5 percent interest a month. When they had bought their "good" used car six months before, they didn't understand that the 10.5 percent interest was "add-on interest" which made it amount to 21 percent annual rate.

The easy credit wasn't easy any more. They played the dart board game to decide what not to pay each month. But by the time they took care of what they could not skip and paid the insurance, utilities, and medical expenses, the money was gone. They were broke all the time.

Bill and Mary came for counseling during a seminar on family money management. We learned some interesting things as we studied together. Here is what we charted:

Obligations	Amount owed	Monthly payment	Annual interest rate	Interest cost per year	Pay out time
Furniture	$1,200	$ 50	12%	$116	2½ yrs.
Store A	350	35	18	63	revolving
Store B	80	10	18	14	revolving
Oil credit card A	150	15	18	27	revolving
Oil credit card B	75	10	18	14	revolving
Oil credit card C	120	15	18	22	revolving
Bank credit card A	400	20	18	72	revolving
Bank credit card B	350	20	18	63	revolving
Car loan	1,800	155	21	210	1½ yrs.
	$4,525	$330		$601*	

*The figures used here and in the rest of the book are based on 1974-75. They should be adjusted to reflect any significant changes that have occurred.

They listed their other monthly expenses as $406, making a total of $736 a month. But they had no provision for medical and dental expenses, clothing, contributions, and several lesser items which apparently had been left out to balance expenditures with their take-home pay of $740 a month. When needs in those areas came up, they had to handle them as emergencies. They had an unrealistic savings goal of over $100 a month, but for obvious reasons weren't putting any money in the bank.

The story of Bill and Mary is not an exaggerated, hypothetical case. It's a real story about real people. Millions of American families, in their desire to have more and more, have found that *things* have not brought them freedom, but bondage.

A million Americans went into bankruptcy from 1967 through 1973, according to financial columnist Richard John Pietschmann. Easy credit is the culprit, he says, in the May 1974 issue of *Mainliner*, the magazine of United Airlines. He estimates that twenty million American families qualify for bankruptcy, for their liabilities exceed their assets.

But most people don't take bankruptcy unless they are so hopelessly in debt that there is no other way. Christians who have a clear ethical concept based on the New Testament will probably feel they must keep the commitments they have made rather than see their obligations so easily dissolved. They may prefer to use Chapter XIII of the Bankruptcy Act by which they can pay off their debts under the direction of a court-appointed trustee.

But there's a better way. You can plan for and achieve financial freedom by following the simple steps suggested in this book. Bill and Mary are doing it. In an extended counseling session we worked out a plan that got them started on the road to financial freedom.

Joe and Debbie have already done it. They weren't in as deep as Bill and Mary, but there were several complicating factors. They had revolving charge accounts with one chain department store and two bank credit cards which totaled about $1,000 at 18 percent annual interest. The accounts tended to grow as they added on a little more than they paid off most of the time. They were overinsured, with a special problem involving an endowment policy on their preschool daughter sold to them to provide for the girl's education. I pointed out that if you want to guarantee your children's education, you don't insure the children, but the father. He already had a good insurance program.

They had bought a suit for Joe on a lay away plan. When I heard they had paid $150 for it I asked, "Why are you paying $150 for a suit, when you can hardly take care of your necessities?"

We spent five hours together, broken by an extended conversation between the two of them. They agreed to a plan that included regular tithing, saving, and debt elimination. Five months later he glowingly reported, "We're out of debt and have $600 in the bank. We went shopping the other night and bought all our Christmas decorations, and it's not even October yet."

They had gone to the store where they had bought the suit on lay away and had gotten back the $30 they had paid on it. He later got just as good a suit from an outlet store for $75 and paid cash. They cashed in their daughter's insurance policy. That gave them a little money to apply on their debts and reduced their monthly obligation. Now they can decide what to do with their money. They are no longer locked into an expensive credit program that dictates their financial decisions.

Do you have financial freedom? Before you answer, we should ask, What is financial freedom? Everyone probably has an idea. In fact, if you ask twelve people you could get thirteen answers. Here are some things it means:

1. No overdue bills
2. No embarrassment because of bills
3. A buffer fund
4. Adequate insurance
   a. Life
   b. Medical and hospital
   c. Disability
5. A good retirement plan
6. Realistic financial goals
7. Freedom to give generously to God's work

Do you have that kind of freedom? Or has credit got you trapped? Would you like to have all the money you need?

"Who wouldn't?" you say. "Just a little more would do it. If I could get a second job, or if my wife would go back to work we could make it."

You're wrong. More income is hardly ever the answer to family financial problems. Unless we take good care of what we get we will never have enough. Without a financial plan we tend to live up to the limit of our income, or beyond. We mortgage our future with credit commitments. Changes in health and jobs can bring fiscal catastrophe. Inflation puts us in the squeeze as prices rise. How much we make isn't nearly as important as what we do with it.

A national television documentary told the story of two families, both of which were successful in getting the things they wanted. But the husbands had two jobs and the wives worked. In one family the husband and wife worked at night while the children stayed home alone. Did they have financial freedom, or were they bound by the love of things?

To help you decide if you have financial freedom, use this check list:

Financial Freedom Check List

	Yes	No	
1.	___	___	Do we know how much we owe on every loan and purchase?
2.	___	___	Do we know how much interest (annual percentage rate) we pay on each obligation?
3.	___	___	Do we know how much our total debt is?
4.	___	___	Do we know what we would do if we had no income for six months?
5.	___	___	Do we have a regular savings plan, and do we save something every payday?
6.	___	___	Do we have adequate medical and hospitalization insurance?
7.	___	___	Do we have a budget for our income and expenses?
8.	___	___	Do we know how we are going to pay for our children's education?
9.	___	___	Do we have provisions for retirement in addition to Social Security?
10.	___	___	Do we have wills to care for our family and to include the Lord's work?
11.	___	___	Do we understand that we are stewards of all God gives, and thus avoid the dangers of materialism?
12.	___	___	Do we give at least 10 percent of our income to the Lord's work in recognition of the ownership of God?
13.	___	___	Do we involve the whole family in our financial planning?
14.	___	___	Do all members of the family have allowances; do they know what the allowances cover and what their family responsibilities are?

How did you come out? Do you need any help? If you do and are willing to receive it, you've taken the first step toward financial freedom.

CHAPTER 2

WHERE DO YOU WANT TO GO?

The plight of a family trying to find its way to financial
freedom may seem something like the story of the motorist
who got lost on a country road. He met a farmer and asked
him how to get where he wanted to go. After several stumbling
attempts to give the complicated directions, the farmer finally
said, "Mister, you just can't get there from here."

That's not true. You can find your way to financial freedom from anywhere. No matter where you are, there's a
way out.

But first, you have to know where you want to go. That's

more important than knowing where you are. Unless you
have a specific destination in mind you will continue to
wander. If you spend too much time analyzing your present
situation before you decide where you want to go you may
feel overwhelmed. A clear sense of direction will help you
avoid that feeling and will give thrust to your financial planning. This chapter will help you define your purpose and set
your goals.

You start with your attitude. If you think you can never get
your financial house in order, you probably won't. If you
believe you are doomed to wander in the wilderness of in-
sufficiency, all your mental powers will subconsciously work
to make it happen. But if you believe there's a way out, and
if you are determined to find it, your mental resources will
work night and day to help you.

So start with a "possibility" attitude. Believe you can do
it. Believe God will help you do it. Then add a generous por-
tion of imagination. Visualize the joy of no unpaid bills and
a growing savings account. Imagine yourself as a generous
supporter of God's work. All your mental and spiritual powers
will work together, with God's help, to bring to reality the
image you hold in your mind.

You'll need a few simple supplies to work out your financial
plan. You should have an 8½x11-inch loose-leaf binder.
One with rings not more than one inch across works best. Get
a package of ruled paper to fit the binder.

You'll also need a twelve-column bookkeeping pad, 8½ x
11-inches, side-opening, punched to fit the binder. We use
number G7212D published by Wilson Jones. Be sure you get
one that has a date column and an item column as well as
twelve regular columns. You'll start using it in chapter 3 and
will use it further when you set up your budget.

Let's get under way. If you don't have the binder and ruled
paper, don't wait. You can start with a plain sheet of paper.

At the top write OUR FINANCIAL PLAN. At the left margin put "I. Purpose." Under that describe the purpose of your financial plan. It could be as simple as, "To find financial freedom as outlined in chapter 1." You may want to spell it out in more detail. You can include specific projects like paying off your debts, buying a home, building up a retirement fund, and providing for your children's education. But don't get too explicit here. We're going to work on goals later. What you want now are the reasons you're working on a plan for financial freedom. Talk it over with your family. Pray about it. Write several drafts. Then put down in one short paragraph what you all agree on as the real purpose of your plan.

When that's done, write "II. Goals" at the left margin. But don't put anything under it, yet. You have some other work to do. Take another sheet of paper, either ruled or plain. Write "Goals" at the top. Beginning at the right edge draw vertical lines to make five columns about one-half inch wide. Label them: (beginning with the left one) Six Months, One Year, Two Years, Five Years, Beyond. This is your work sheet to help you sort out your goals.

If it's hard to decide when you want to reach certain goals, don't let it worry you. Just write them down. Don't bother with the time element now. Start anywhere. Let the whole family get in on it. List as many as you can; you'll get more good ones that way. Use as many pages as you need.

Go back over what you've written and evaluate your goals. Remember that goals should be accomplishable, measurable, and challenging. They should fit your purpose. Any that do not meet those standards should be dropped. You may find you can combine some. Others may not seem important when compared with the purpose you have decided upon. Get right down to the basics of what you really want to do with your money.

Now you're ready to develop a schedule. Study each goal carefully, whether it's the payment of a debt, the building of a savings account, or a major purchase. Check a column for each goal, according to when you plan to reach it. You may need to divide some so you can take them in steps.

Transfer the information from the work sheet to your financial plan sheet. Indent under "II. Goals" and write "Six Months." Indent again and list your six-month goals. Repeat the process for the other time segments till all your goals are listed.

When you finish, you'll know where you're headed. You'll also begin to see the road that leads to financial freedom. Keep your eyes on that road and you'll get where you want to go.

Eventually you must do more with your "Beyond" list. You'll want to set specific long-range goals relating to retirement, family education, housing, and other matters. Some of your strategy will develop as you work on your overall plans. We'll deal with some of the details in subsequent chapters.

As you set your financial goals you should work for a well-rounded plan with proper priorities. It's easy to say, "We just want to get out of debt." That's a good objective, but it won't give you financial freedom if it stands alone.

Many believe they should not plan to save till their debts are paid. "How can we save when we have so many bills?" they ask. The answer is simple. You owe yourself something of everything you make. So pay yourself first. If you don't, you'll never save. And you'll probably not get out of debt either. Chapter 6 will tell you how to put it all together.

Be sure you set goals for the support of the work of the Lord. Every Christian should include God in all his financial plans.

Debt-related goals should be double-headed. First, set schedules to pay off what you owe. Then, make plans to save money that you can use to pay cash for what you buy. You'll save the interest on the credit purchases, and receive interest on the money you save. By reversing the flow of interest, you start it working for you rather than against you.

When you get goals set for your present needs and future plans you will have taken a big step. So plan well, and plan realistically. The best way to do that is to use your imagination. Visualize a life of financial freedom. Dream of the day when you'll pay all your bills on time. Imagine the joy of paying cash for the car and the furniture you need. Carry your imagination further. Picture the steps you need to take to reach your goals. Take a positive attitude and commit yourself to the fulfillment of your plans. When you do that, your whole being will press toward the accomplishment of what you are determined to do.

CHAPTER 3

WHERE ARE YOU?

You can solve almost any financial problem if you put pencil to paper. You started that when you defined your purpose and set your goals. Your next step is to find out where you are right now.

A little boy wailing in a department store finally subsided so a grandmotherly customer could communicate with him. "Are you lost, honey?" she asked.

"No, I'm not lost," he said. "My mommy's lost and I can't find her."

If you don't know where you are, you're lost. That's true

geographically, spiritually, and financially. You can't measure your progress toward your goals unless you know where you want to go, where you started from, and where you are.

Here's where you start to use the columnar pad I referred to in chapter 2. But if you don't have it, don't wait to get started. Just use a plain sheet of paper and follow the sample forms on page 28.

Under assets list everything you own that is of value using the realistic present market value; check the classified ads for what houses and cars are selling for. Your bank can give you the value of your car according to the National Automobile Dealers Association. Don't forget to include furniture, appliances, and personal belongings of value.

For insurance, you want the present cash value of all policies on all members of your family. You can usually get this from a chart printed on the policy, probably by the value per one thousand dollars of insurance and the number of years you've held it. Since term insurance is for protection only it does not have cash value. If you have questions ask the agent for the company that wrote the policy to help you.

Carefully complete your list of assets and add it up. Include anything you have in a retirement plan, but not Social Security. You'll use it to calculate your retirement income, but other values vary too much to use it as a present asset.

Now it's time to put down your liabilities. Include mortgages, personal and auto loans, contracts, charge accounts, medical and dental bills, and everything else you owe any company or person. Don't omit what you may owe to relatives or friends. If you have school bills owed to colleges, banks, or the government, include them. Don't be afraid to put it all down. You need to look every obligation straight in the face, see exactly what it looks like, and make plans to take care of it. If you ignore it, it will probably hit you over the head when you're least prepared to handle it.

Add up your liabilities. Enter the assets as shown on page 28 and subtract the liabilities. The difference is your net worth. If your liabilities exceed your assets put parentheses around the final figures to show that you owe more than you own. If you're in the hole, don't try to cover it up. You'll never get out if you don't admit you're in, just like the sinner who can't find forgiveness because he won't admit he needs it. Whether your net worth comes out black or red, praise God because you're on your way, and move ahead.

The process you're going through will open up communication and understanding between husband and wife, and with other members of the family. I remember Ed and Angie. Their case seemed simple compared to many. Although they weren't saving any money and had a few embarrassing bills, they had a rather small total debt load. But as we talked, both told of bills the other didn't know about. We developed a plan to get their debts paid off and start a savings program. The session opened up communication between them concerning their finances. They now share a common concern and are working together to meet the goals they've set for themselves. (Please see charts on next page.)

How Much Are We Worth?

Assets	Description	Value
House		$
Other real estate		
Car(s)		
Other vehicles		
Furniture		
Life insurance (cash value)		
Savings accounts		
Other savings		
Checking accounts		
Bonds and securities		
Retirement plan (present value)		
Annuities		
Other assets		
Total		$

Liabilities	Description	Value
Mortgage(s)		$
Personal loans		
Car loan(s)		
Installment contracts		
Charge accounts		
Credit cards		
Medical and dental		
Other		
Total		$

Total assets $

Total liabilities $

(subtract)

Net worth $

CHAPTER 4

IT ALL BELONGS TO GOD

The committed Christian doesn't own anything. He manages money for God. A workable approach to Christian financial planning must begin with a clear understanding of that fact.

When we became Christians we entered into a relationship with God. Paul made that plain when he said, "Do you not know that your body is a temple of the Holy Spirit within you, which you have from God? You are not your own; you were bought with a price. So glorify God in your body" (1 Cor. 6:19, 20). God paid an extravagant price for our redemption; he sent his own Son to die for us. In the light of that divine extravagance Paul wrote, "I appeal to you therefore, brethren, by the mercies of God, to present your bodies as a living sacrifice, holy and acceptable to God (Rom. 12:1).

If we recognize the ownership of God we will demonstrate it by our stewardship. That means we put God first. Dr. Stephen Olford says, "We can talk until doomsday about being surrendered Christians, but we virtually lie until we give evidence of our surrender through our stewardship."

Ananias and Sapphira made a fatal mistake with their money. Acts 5 tells their story. They saw others sell their possessions and give the proceeds to help the believers who suffered financial persecution because of their faith. After talking it over they decided to sell a field and give part of the money. When Peter asked if what they gave was the total they had received, they said it was. Peter's piercing question "How is it that you have contrived this deed in your heart?" was never answered. They both died on the spot.

Why did they lie to God? Was it because they wanted credit for generosity without paying the price? Did they think they could have the benefits of the fellowship without being fully open? Interesting questions, but we will profit more by answering them for ourselves rather than for them.

Why did God use money to bring us this potent lesson from the early church? Probably because our possessions are so critical in our relations with God and with man. Money has no moral value in itself; it takes on moral qualities by the way it is handled. Our attitude toward our money and our use of it makes it a blight or a blessing.

In the Sermon on the Mount Jesus said, "Where your treasure is, there will your heart be also." No matter how much or how little money you have, you can lay up treasure in heaven. Here's how:

1. Recognize that all you are and all you have belongs to God.

2. Seek his will in everything you do, including your giving.
3. Obey him, and you'll find the way to joyful living and giving.

The Bible gives us guidelines for giving. Paul wrote to the Christians at Corinth, "On the first day of every week, each of you is to put something aside and store it up, as he may prosper, so that contributions need not be made when I come" (1 Cor. 16:2).

That simple formula suggests we should give regularly, personally, and proportionately rather than under pressure. What we give is to be laid aside before we pay our bills or buy our groceries. We put God first.

Some five centuries before the law of God was given through Moses, an incident occurred that relates to giving. Abraham had joined with local chieftains to rescue Lot, his nephew, with the women and goods that had been carried away by the Elamites. On his return he was blessed by Melchizedek, the priest-king of Salem. Abraham then gave Melchizedek a tenth of all the spoils (Gen. 14:20; Heb. 9:2-6). About 200 years later Jacob promised God to tithe in gratitude for God's favor (Gen. 28:22). Both cases were voluntary expressions of praise. Their actions imply the probability of a rather general acceptance of tithing by pious Hebrews. When the Law was given it took the already established principle and practice and made them a part of worship, service, and daily living.

What did Jesus say about it? Three things.

First, he made it clear he did not come into the world to do away with the Law. He said, "Think not that I have come to abolish the law and the prophets; I have not come to abolish them but to fulfil them" (Matt. 5:17). His fulfillment, in every case, goes beyond the Law.

The ceremonial laws relating to sacrifice were superseded by his sacrifice of himself. The laws regarding the priesthood were fulfilled in him, the Great High Priest, and the priest-hood of believers by which we all have access to God through Christ. The Ten Commandments cut much closer in the light of his interpretation of them in the Sermon on the Mount. The sanctity of marriage is lifted above culture and custom by his indictment of the lustful look and the chauvinistic putting away of a wife. He moved from the sin of the overt act to the sin of the inner attitude.

Second, Christ commended tithing. He said, "Woe to you, scribes and Pharisees, hypocrites! for you tithe mint and dill and cummin, and have neglected the weightier matters of the law, justice and mercy and faith . . ." If he had stopped there, perhaps we could conclude he didn't care much about tithing. But he didn't stop. He went on, " . . . these you ought to have done, without neglecting the others" (Matt. 23:23).

Third, he set a standard for giving that goes beyond the tithe. And he linked it with acceptance and forgiveness to form a triad of Christian graces. He said, "Judge not, and you will not be judged; condemn not, and you will not be condemned; forgive, and you will be forgiven; give, and it will be given to you; good measure, pressed down, shaken together, running over, will be put into your lap. For the measure you give will be the measure you get back" (Luke 6:37, 38).

When he said, "Give and it will be given to you," he intro-duced a new relationship between giving and receiving. Jacob said, "As the Lord blesses me, I will tithe." Jesus said, "First give, then you will receive." That kind of openhandedness, in the spiritual climate of acceptance and forgiveness, helps us become cheerful givers, whom God loves.

Jesus used an object lesson to nail down his teaching on giving and receiving. He sat where he could watch the people put their money into the offering box. The wealthy put in large amounts. Then came a poor widow who put in two copper coins. He called his disciples to him and said, "Truly,

I say to you, this poor widow has put in more than all those who are contributing to the treasury. For they all contributed out of their abundance; but she out of her poverty has put in everything she had, her whole living" (Mark 12:43, 44).

How foolish can a woman be? She had so little and she gave it all away. How did she expect to live? She had faith in the one who said, "Give, and it will be given to you."

When Paul wrote to the Corinthians to encourage their generosity, he used the churches of Macedonia as examples. He said, "We want you to know, brethren, about the grace of God which has been shown to the churches of Macedonia, for in a severe test of affliction, their abundance of joy and their extreme poverty have overflowed in a wealth of liberality on their part. For they gave according to their means, as I can testify, and beyond their means, of their own free will, begging us earnestly for the favor of taking part" (2 Cor. 8:1-4). They were joyful, giving, going churches. They took the risk of faith as they gave out of their poverty and joy. It's hard to find a gloomy open-handed Christian or a happy close-fisted one.

CHAPTER 5

IT'S A FAMILY AFFAIR

Who takes care of the money at your house? That's not a good question, for there's no right answer to it. Unless you say, "We all do." Money management is a family affair.

That may jolt some men who think they should have all the responsibility and all of the authority for handling the family money. Or others who would like to have their wives take care of it all. And some parents who don't think the children should have any part in it. But, without denying the proper leadership role of husbands and fathers, you need to involve everyone in the business of the family.

"But," some ask, "doesn't the Bible teach that the husband-father should have full charge of the money?"

That concept is based on Old Testament models and reinforced with New Testament references such as, "Wives, be subject to your husbands . . ." (Eph. 5:22). But serious cultural, scriptural, and practical difficulties face families that try to follow it.

Most of the cultural crust of Old Testament family life has fallen away. We don't practice polygamy; we don't barter brides; grown children don't stay home as a part of family kingdoms. But the basic principle of family life remains in a stronger form. The sanctity of Christian marriage involves a one-to-one relationship for life.

But what about Ephesians 5:22? Doesn't it teach that wives should be in subjection to their husbands?

Not really.

Its use to try to prove the unlimited authority of husbands shows the error we can fall into when we use fragments of Scripture out of context to proof-text a position. When you look at the entire passage you get a very different picture.

The previous verse sets the basis for all human relationships with, "Be subject one to another out of reverence for Christ." Then verses 22 through 24 speak directly to wives:

> Wives, be subject to your husbands, as to the Lord. For the husband is the head of the wife as Christ is the head of the church, his body, and is himself its Savior. As the church is subject to Christ, so let wives also be subject in everything to their husbands.

But verses 25 to 28 lay a heavier responsibility on husbands:

> Husbands, love your wives, as Christ loved the church and gave himself up for her, that he might sanctify her, having cleansed her by the washing of water with the word, that he might present the

church to himself in splendor, without spot or wrinkle or any such thing, that she might be holy and without blemish. Even so husbands should love their wives as their own bodies. He who loves his wife loves himself.

It sums up husband-wife relationships with, "However, let each one of you love his wife as himself, and let the wife see that she respects her husband" (v. 33).

Ephesians 6:1 then turns to children. "Children, obey your parents in the Lord, for this is right. 'Honor your father and mother' [this is the first commandment with a promise] that it may be well with you and that you may live long on the earth."

But to fathers verse 4 says, "Fathers, do not provoke your children to anger, but bring them up in the discipline and instruction of the Lord."

Out of the consideration of these Scriptures emerges the clear fact that the husband-wife relationship is a partnership. Family life is a cooperative endeavor; it involves everyone. Husbands should carry the major responsibility for the leadership of the home, including finance. But he does himself a disfavor and severely handicaps the other members of the family if he tries to do it all himself. Husbands and wives should talk freely and openly about their financial affairs. They should have no secrets. Engaged couples should include finance in their planning. Children should be involved in family financial matters as they are able to understand and participate.

My twenty-three-year-old friend, Dave Brown, told me how it was in his family. They had very little when he was growing up. Some nights they had only pancakes and rice for supper. There was never enough money to go around. It was tough for him, but tougher for his older brother, Joe.

Joe never knew why he couldn't have what he wanted. He was not involved in the family financial matters. He saw what others had and felt deprived. He became resentful and rebellious.

After a hitch in the service he came out and got a good job. His income was adequate, but he had a ravenous hunger for possessions. Since he never understood why his parents didn't let him have all the things he wanted, he decided he would have them now. He overspent and got into deep financial trouble to the point of bankruptcy.

Dave's parents handled it differently with him; perhaps because they saw their mistakes with Joe. They let Dave know just what their situation was. He understood why he could not have many things he wanted. When he had to quit the high school band and go to work, he did so without resentment.

I asked Dave, "Do you think the difference was because your parents let you know what the situation was and they didn't with your brother?"

"I think that was it," he said. "He never understood because they never let him in on their financial situation."

CHAPTER 6

BUDGETS CAN BE FUN

When you start to talk about budgets some people want to run away and hide. They think budgets are burdens that take the fun out of life. They see a budget book as a strait jacket that restricts your life and makes a miserable miser of you.

But budgets don't need to be like that. A budget properly used won't enslave you; it will set you free. It doesn't take money away from you; it gives you more money to use for what you want. And since it involves keeping an accurate record, it helps you know where you stand and what progress you're making toward your goals.

The best way to handle a budget is to make a game of it. Not a frivolous game, but a serious one, for you're playing for keeps. As a family you can watch your progress, plan your strategy, and adapt to changing situations. If you run into financial trouble, you don't give up; you face it as a family and work out plans to handle it. And you ask God to help you, for he still works miracles.

Where do you start? You've already started if you followed through with the suggestions in chapter 3. You know where you are. You know what you own and what you owe. If you haven't completed that work, do it now. You can't move on till you have.

The next step is to list your income and expenses. How do you do that?

Let's build a family model to help us. Wilbur and Mary Johnson are thirty-four and thirty-two years old. They have three children: Susan, sixteen; Bill, twelve; and Linda, six. Wilbur's gross pay is $785 a month; Mary's is $565. Susan babysits and averages about $30 a month. Bill has a paper route that pays him $28. We'll work with the Johnsons as our model, but you should use your own family.

You need to know what your total income is. Do it this way:

Our Monthly Income

WILBUR:
Salary	$785	
Bonus (1/12th of $500)	42	
		$827

MARY:
Salary	565

SUSAN:
Babysitting	30	
Gifts	4	
		34

BILL:

Paper route	28	
Gifts	3	
		31

OTHER INCOME:

Gifts to family	10	
Interest income ($500 savings)	2	
		12
Total average monthly income		$1,469
Less children's personal income		65
Family income before taxes and other deductions		$1,404

As you put together the statement of your family's average monthly income, be sure you include everything. You want it to be:

1. Complete
2. A monthly average
3. Total pay before taxes and other deductions

If you have any other income, be sure you list it. You may wonder about including the earnings of the children. Isn't that theirs? Yes, but you need to get the whole picture. And their income will influence your budgeting as you consider their total needs. We've taken it out at the bottom to show the net regular family income.

Income of $1,404 a month looks pretty good, but before they get any of it $263 comes out for federal and state taxes, social security, and health insurance. The Johnsons can live rather well on the $1,141 that's left if they handle it right. And you can live on your income if you believe you can and if you will really work at it.

Now comes the hard part. You need to list all of your expenditures. Start with your checkbook. Go over it for the last twelve months. Use your columnar pad or a sheet of plain paper to make a listing according to the breakdown below.

What about your cash expenditures? Getting them listed will take some memory sessions. Let yourself float back over the last twelve months in a blending of memory and imagination. Since imagination is memory projected and memory is imagination past, you can effectively use them together. Imagine yourself through the year, month by month and week by week. You'll find your memory coming alive. Have some family sessions and some private ones. Remember that you want the monthly average. Be sure you don't leave anything out. Add it all up and enter under "Monthly Average Last Twelve Months" on your expenditure plan.

Our Expenditure Plan

	Monthly Average Last 12 months	Monthly Average Next 12 months
Fixed expenditures		
Tithe	_____	_____
Savings	_____	_____
Insurance		
Life	_____	_____
Health and accident	_____	_____
Property	_____	_____
Taxes	_____	_____
Rent or house payment	_____	_____
Installment payments	_____	_____
	_____	_____	_____
	_____	_____	_____
Total fixed expenditures	_____	_____

Flexible expenditures
    Food (including
        school lunches
        and meals out) _____ _____

    Entertainment _____ _____

    Household operation _____ _____

    Furniture _____ _____

    Housing (repairs and
        improvements) _____ _____

    Clothing and cleaning _____ _____

    Personal allowances _____ _____

    Medical
        Doctor, dentist,
        drugs _____ _____

    Transportation _____ _____

    Education
        School expenses _____ _____

        Music lessons,
        etc. _____ _____

        Books and
        magazines _____ _____

    Recreation _____ _____

    Christmas and other
        gifts _____ _____

    Other expenses

_____ _____

_____ _____

_____ _____

Total flexible expenses _____ _____

GRAND TOTAL _____ _____

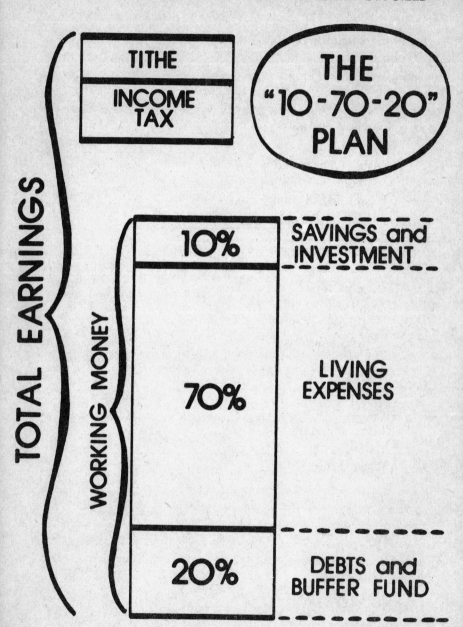

If your expenditures are less than your income, you should have some money in the bank to make the difference. If you don't, maybe you have missed something. If your expenditures are more than your income you should owe more now than you did a year ago or have less savings. You may not be able to catch every dollar, but do the best you can.

What you've done becomes the basis for building your expenditure budget. Some of your expenses are fixed; you can't change them unless you make major changes in your life-style. Others are flexible; you can work with them. You can now see how much adjustment you'll have to make for your income and expenditures to match. You'll make the adjustments in the flexible expenses.

You may question the inclusion of tithe and savings under fixed expenditures. If we accept the fact that God owns all we have and that he requires us to adopt priorities in spending we'll not struggle much over the tithe. It's a witness to our faith in God and loyalty to him. As an act of faith it should be a fixed commitment if your income is regular. Savings should be considered a fixed expense because if we don't save first, we won't save at all.

How can we tithe and save if we have a lot of debts to pay off? George Bowman worked out the 10–70–20 plan in his book, *How to Succeed with Your Money*. He suggests that after tithe and tax a family should put 10 percent of their remaining money in savings, use 70 percent for living expenses, and pay off old debts with 20 percent. When the debts are paid the 20 percent should go to savings and investments. (See chart on page 44.)

I've recommended Mr. Bowman's plan as I've worked with couples in financial difficulty. In many cases we've had to shift the percentages, but the plan has always worked. You may have to cut your savings to 5 percent till you get some things paid off. It may take more than 20 percent to pay off your debts. You may have to live on 65 percent, or even 60. But you should never skip the tithe and you should put something in savings every payday.

What about allowances? Every member of the family should have one; father, mother, and every child when he can understand anything about money. That's one of the most important parts of successful budgeting. Children's allowances should not be given for work they do and should not be withheld as punishment. Each one should receive an allowance because he is a member of the family. He should share in home responsibilities for the same reason. He does regular chores as his contribution to family life. He may be paid extra for special jobs, and he may get outside jobs like Susan and Bill Johnson.

Allowances should increase as children grow older, and should cover more and more of their needs. The enlarging process will give them greater freedom and will teach them how to handle money. They should set up their own budget systems and learn to tithe and to save.

What about allowances for father and mother? We've found they make budgeting livable. We each take $5 a week (I usually suggest that young couples start with less). That's our money. Nobody can tell us what to do with it. We simply show it as "Personal" in our budget book when we take it.

We use our allowances for strictly personal things. I pay for haircuts, shaving lotion, toothpaste, coffee breaks, and other personal items. But I don't use it for anything that fits somewhere else in the budget. I carry a card in my wallet on which I record such expenditures. If we go out to eat and I pay for the meal out of my personal money, I write it on the card, showing date, what it was for, and the amount. When I get home I post it in our book, reimburse myself from the "kitty," and mark it off the card. I do the same for gas, groceries, and anything else that's not a personal expense.

I keep another card in another part of my wallet where I sometimes carry family money. I record what I spend, then post and mark off the card so we have a full record of all expenditures. My wife follows the same procedure.

Let's get back to your expenditure plan. Apply the 10–70–20 approach. Does it fit? Can you meet your present payments on past purchases with 20 percent of your working money after tithe and taxes? You don't need to include house payments; they have their own place in the budget. But all other installment and credit card payments must be considered as old debts.

If 20 percent doesn't cover them you have three options. You can use more for debts and less for living and savings. That will require careful adjustments within your flexible expenses. It may require some sacrifices for a while, but the results will be worth it.

You can contact your creditors and ask for reduction of payments and extension of time. If you do that, try to get the adjustments on the accounts or loans with the lowest interest. Pay off the high interest accounts first. If your debts include college loans with government-subsidized low interest, you should pay them as slowly as possible. If you are paying 3 percent interest you'll be ahead to let the loan run its course and put any extra money you have in savings.

Most firms will react positively to a request for payment adjustment if you can show them you have a definite plan to take care of your obligations. In many cities there are non-profit consumer-credit counseling organizations that can help you. Check your phone book or the Chamber of Commerce. I don't recommend that you go to a commercial credit counselor or a loan company. You may find your obligations increased rather than reduced.

The third, and least desirable, option is to get a consolida-

tion loan. Before you go that way you should know exactly
what will happen. In most cases the time for payment of debts
and the interest rate are increased. It can cost you a lot of
money: be sure you know how much. I don't recommend a
debt consolidation loan if you can find any other way, and
you probably can.

If your expenses are more than your income you'll have to
make some trade-offs. Each member of the family should look
for ways to cut down. You may be surprised how much you'll
save by knowing how much you're spending. If things are
really tight dad may have to give up bowling for a while, mom
may have to do her own hair, and the kids may have to get
along with less. You may need to postpone some purchases
you've planned. That may not sound like much fun, but it's
a lot more fun than getting into debt so deep that you face
real financial disaster. If you cut down now to get out of
debt, you'll soon have more money to spend for what you
want.

When you have your budget all set up, the fun really begins.
You have goals to work for. You know what you want to do
with your money. You can use a thermometer chart if you
want. Put your debt total at the top. If you use a movable
ribbon you can bring it down to zero as you pay off. Then you
can spend some money for a celebration dinner.

To reach that happy situation and move on toward your
other financial goals you will have to keep records. Use your
columnar pad for this, following the example at the end of this
chapter. Write in the categories at the top of the columns.
Put the month and year at the top left. Enter the date for each
item of income and expenditure and the sources of receipts
and the payees for expenditures. Put the amounts in the proper
columns. The list in the "Index to Budget Record" will help
you decide how to categorize various items. If you have any
refunds, such as from insurance on medical expenses or

mileage allowance paid to you, put parentheses around them and subtract from the total of the column.

You may have to use more than one set of pages for a month. You can carry forward in two ways. One is to total at the bottom of the first page and enter the amount from there at the top of the next page. The other way is to add the columns straight through both pages at the end of the month. That works well if you have an adding machine. An inexpensive machine or a small calculator will be a help if its purchase will fit your budget. Small calculators can now be bought for less than $20. One word of caution: if you use a calculator without a tape, check your addition by subtracting out item by item what you have added in. You should come out with zero.

At the end of the month add up all the columns. Write "Total Actual" in the item column on the same line as the totals. On the next line put "Total Planned" then enter what you budgeted for each column. Subtract the smaller from the larger. If "Actual" is more than "Planned" put the balance in parentheses. That means you have overspent and are in the red. But don't panic. You'll need two or three months to see how you are averaging out. Be prepared to adjust your budget as necessary.

Beginning with your second month you will bring forward the balances from the previous month. Label that line "Brought Forward." Add to the balances for the current month, making sure you handle negative figures properly, and you have your up-to-date status.

What if you have a column where you have more credits than expenditures during the month? That represents negative spending. You put parentheses around the figure on the "Total Actual" line. You have money to spare in that category, so you add the amount in the parentheses to the amount you had planned to spend to get your balance.

			Income	Tithe & Contributions
1	1	Payroll (Mom)	99 08	
2	2	Groceries		
3	2	Allowances		
4	2	Gas		
5	3	Our church – Tithe		30 00
6	3	Sunday School Offering		3 00
7	4	Dr. Smith (Bill)		
8	5	Cleaning		
9	6	Electric Bill		
10	7	Payroll (Dad)	328 00	
11	7	First National Bank		
12	8	Payroll (Mom)	99 08	
13	8	Life Insurance (Dad)		
14	9	Groceries		
15	9	Allowances		
16	9	Car Insurance		
17	10	Tithe		30 00
18	10	Missionary Offering		15 00
19	12	House Insurance		
20	14	House Payment		
21	15	Dress (Mom)		
22	15	Piano Lesson		
23	15	Payroll (Mom)	99 08	
24				
25				
26				
27				
28				
29				
30				
31				
32		Total Actual		
33		Total Planned		
34		Balances		
35		Brought Forward		
36		Net Balances		
37				

August, 19––

	3 Savings	4 Life Insurance	5 Other Insurance	6 Taxes	7 Rent or House Payment	8 Food	
1							
2						38 20	
3							
4							
5							
6							
7							
8							
9							
10							
11	45 00						
12							
13		55 00					
14						32 20	
15							
16							
17							
18							
19				110 00			
20					142 30		
21							
22							
23							
24							
25							
26							
27							
28							
29							
30							
31							
32							
33							
34							
35							
36							
37							

	House Operation	Repairs & Improvements	Furniture	Clothing	Personal	Medical
1						
2						
3					1250	
4						
5						
6						
7						1500
8				170		
9	2380					
10						
11						
12						
13						
14						
15					1250	
16						
17						
18						
19						
20						
21				3840		
22						
23						
24						
25						
26						
27						
28						
29						
30						
31						
32						
33						
34						
35						
36						
37						

...rs & ...vements	Furniture	Clothing	Personal	Medical
			1250	
				1500
		170		
			1250	
		3840		

mileage allowance paid to you, put parentheses around them and subtract from the total of the column.

You may have to use more than one set of pages for a month. You can carry forward in two ways. One is to total at the bottom of the first page and enter the amount from there at the top of the next page. The other way is to add the columns straight through both pages at the end of the month. That works well if you have an adding machine. An inexpensive machine or a small calculator will be a help if its purchase will fit your budget. Small calculators can now be bought for less than $20. One word of caution: if you use a calculator without a tape, check your addition by subtracting out item by item what you have added in. You should come out with zero.

At the end of the month add up all the columns. Write "Total Actual" in the item column on the same line as the totals. On the next line put "Total Planned" then enter what you budgeted for each column. Subtract the smaller from the larger. If "Actual" is more than "Planned" put the balance in parentheses. That means you have overspent and are in the red. But don't panic. You'll need two or three months to see how you are averaging out. Be prepared to adjust your budget as necessary.

Beginning with your second month you will bring forward the balances from the previous month. Label that line "Brought Forward." Add to the balances for the current month, making sure you handle negative figures properly, and you have your up-to-date status.

What if you have a column where you have more credits than expenditures during the month? That represents negative spending. You put parentheses around the figure on the "Total Actual" line. You have money to spare in that category, so you add the amount in the parentheses to the amount you had planned to spend to get your balance.

August, 19--

			Income	Tithe & Contributions	Savings	Life Insurance	...Insurance	House Operation	Repairs/Improvements
1	1	Payroll (Mom)	99 08						
2	2	Groceries							
3	2	Allowances							
4	2	Gas							
5	3	Our church Tithe		30 00					
6	3	Sunday School Offering		3 00					
7	4	Dr. Smith (Bill)							
8	5	Cleaning							
9	6	Electric Bill						23 80	
10	7	Payroll (Dad)	328 00						
11	7	First National Bank							
12	8	Payroll (Mom)	99 08		45 00				
13	8	Life Insurance (Dad)				55 00			
14	9	Groceries							
15	9	Allowances							
16	9	Car Insurance							
17	10	Tithe		30 00					
18	10	Missionary Offering		15 00					
19	12	House Insurance							
20	14	House Payment							
21	15	Dress (Mom)							
22	15	Piano Lesson							
23	15	Payroll (Mom)	99 08						
24									
25									
26									
27									
28									
29									
30									
31									
32		Total Actual							
33		Total Planned							
34		Balances							
35		Brought Forward							
36		Net Balances							
37									

	15	16	17	18	19	20	
	Trans-portation	Education	Recreation	Gifts to Others	Christmas	Misc.	
1							
2							
3							
4	482						
5							
6							
7							
8							
9							
10							
11							
12							
13							
14							
15							
16	8500						
17							
18							
19							
20							
21							
22		1500					
23							
24							
25							
26							
27							
28							
29							
30							
31							
32							
33							
34							
35							
36							
37							

CHAPTER 7

THE CREDIT TRAP

Howard and Mabel had very little when they got married. But they soon learned they could get almost anything they wanted on credit.

That's how they got their first car. It gave them a lot of trouble so they traded it in for another one. The friendly dealer arranged long-term financing and they didn't bother to ask about the interest and insurance costs. That one was turned in on a new car, which was eventually replaced by another one. When it became troublesome they found it had depreciated faster than they were paying it off. They had no equity, but they found a dealer who "helped" them get a good used sedan. More than a year later, when it needed some work, they considered trading again. It was then that they realized they had signed two contracts; one for financing on the car and another for the down payment. All their payments to that time had gone to the second note. Since the car had depreciated they still owed more on it than it was worth.

In the meantime, they had used credit to get other things they wanted, such as furniture, a camera, clothes, and travel. As the payments mounted up, they refinanced some obligations several times, with ever-increasing interest rates. They were paying over 30 percent on some of their debts.

Howard and Mabel are not rare exceptions in family finance. They are a composite of couples I have counseled who have been in deep financial trouble because they did not understand the price of interest. They represent millions of families who use credit to the hilt. They play the game of credit roulette, hoping they will not get caught. In Russian roulette the player puts one cartridge in a revolver, and spins the cylinder. Then he puts the gun to his head and pulls the trigger. The odds are five-to-one he will win.

When you play credit roulette you have less chance of winning. Every credit purchase increases the risk. As you overextend yourself, you put more bullets in the gun. If you continue, you come to financial suicide.

It's too easy to buy what you want when you want it. You sign contracts and pay high interest. You find you don't have enough money to go around so you begin to juggle your payments and get "consolidation loans." You may pay 20 to 30 percent or more interest on them. You are "hooked" on credit. You will never be free unless you take the "cure."

Good income will not guarantee that you will not get caught in the credit trap. The *National Observer* has reported that families with good credit ratings and substantial incomes have found that inflation has wiped out their discretionary income.

Families caught in the credit trap seldom know what it costs them. It costs plenty. And because of differences in the calculation of interest rates and other credit-related charges, the consumer often doesn't know how big a bite financing is taking. My secretary learned that.

On a hot June day she and her husband decided they would get the room air conditioner they had been talking about. They had money in their savings account, but didn't want to take it out.

"Could we get it now and pay for it at the end of the month?" they asked the dealer.

"No problem at all," he responded. "We'll just write up a regular contract and if you pay it off within thirty days, there'll be no interest charge."

So they went ahead. Here's how the dealer wrote it up:

Purchase price	$219.95
Sales tax	8.80
Cash price	228.75
Down payment	28.75
Unpaid balance	200.00
Credit property insurance premium	8.18
Credit life insurance premium	7.07
Credit disability insurance premium	8.90
Amount financed	224.15
Finance charge	67.67
(21% annual rate)	
Total payments	291.82
Deferred payment price	320.57

To be paid in 30 payments of $9.20 per month and a final payment that may vary slightly, but will not be more than twice the regular monthly payment.

That final payment would have been $14.32 if they had used the full 31-month payment plan. You can see that it would have cost them $91.82 to finance a balance of $200. That would have increased the cost of the air conditioner by 41.7 percent.

They paid it off at the end of the month as they planned and all the insurance and finance charges were rebated. But if they hadn't, they would have limited their purchasing power by the amount of the extra charges. And what's more, the contract provided for add-on privileges. Too many families get started on that kind of credit spending and never get out of debt.

One day when I was discussing credit buying with some friends, one of them asked, "How much debt should a family have?"

"Zero," I answered.

As they began to recover from my radical response they asked me what I meant. I explained that I know credit is sometimes necessary, but a family should set zero debt as its goal and make it a reality as soon as possible. When it is necessary to borrow or buy on credit they should shop for the financing as carefully as they shop for the merchandise.

The purchase of a home is the largest expenditure most families make. The transience of modern society has reduced its significance, and increased costs of construction and financing have lowered its desirability. Families have turned more and more to apartment complexes that have grown like mushrooms around our cities.

Because of the mobility of society and the cost of home ownership you will want to weigh carefully whether you should buy or rent. If you expect to stay where you are for twenty years or more, if you can buy at the right price, and if you can get financing at a reasonable rate you probably are wise to buy. But in today's market you should be able to pay one-third or more down and should not pay more than 8 percent interest on the mortgage. That stops most people. Some find homes they can buy where they can take over an existing mortgage at less than 8 percent. With sufficient down payment they can safely go ahead.

But it has now been proved that in most cases it is cheaper to rent than to own. The big question is what you do with what you save. If you use it carelessly you lose the advantage, but if you save it you will come out ahead.

To avoid the credit trap you need to understand about the different kinds of interest. The most desirable is simple interest, by which the charge is always figured on the unpaid balance. For example, you may borrow $1,000 and agree to pay it at $100 per month including principal and interest at 10 percent per year. The first month your interest charge is one-twelfth of 10 percent of $1,000, or $8.33. That much of your $100 payment is your interest cost for that month. The balance of $91.67 applies to the principal, reducing it to $908.67. The next month you pay one-twelfth of ten percent of the new balance, which will amount to $7.57. Each month the interest is less and the principal payment is more. The actual amount of interest paid is approximately one-half of the interest rate, because of the declining balance on which it is figured.

Federal law now requires that interest rates be clearly stated on all contracts. The charges must be given in terms of simple interest, even though they may be calculated on some other basis. The law also requires the use of the simple rate in quotations of charges given by lenders and merchants. But they don't always do it. I've tried it out on automobile salesmen and department stores. Only rarely have I been given the true annual rate. Usually they've quoted the "add-on" rate, which sounds good, but costs much more.

What is add-on interest? It's a percentage of the amount financed that is added on to the principal at the time the contract is written. The total is then divided by the number of months the contract is to run to get the amount to be paid each month. And there may be some other add-ons.

I checked it out recently. A compact car well loaded with optional equipment priced out at $4,946. The dealer offered me $1,200 for my car in trade. Here's how it looked:

Purchase price	$4,946
Sales tax (4% of difference)	150
Cash price with tax	5,096
Trade in	1,200
Balance due	3,896
Installment credit insurance	90
Amount financed	3,986
Finance charge	
(7% add-on—14% annual rate)	837
Deferred payment price	6,023
Payments: $134 per month for	
36 months	

The financing with the credit insurance, which would pay off the car if I should die, adds almost 20 percent to the price. And I would be locked in, for the interest would be charged in advance. I wouldn't get full credit if I paid off the contract early. That was for bank financing. A loan company would have been even more.

I know how it works for I used to do it. Cars weren't as expensive then, but incomes weren't as high either. I drove 30,000 to 35,000 miles a year and changed cars every year. I justified it on the basis of the amount of driving I did and the mileage money I got. But my balance kept climbing and so did the interest rates. I finally got simple interest financing and changed to compact cars. But it wasn't till we got started on our own zero debt program that we learned how to buy a car with our own money.

The April 1974 issue of *Consumer Reports* carried an interesting article about "How to Shop for an Auto Loan."

You'll find it worthwhile to look it up, but let me share three interesting things from it.

First, if you must finance a car, borrow as little as you can get by with and make arrangements to pay it off as quickly as you can. You'll save money that way.

Second, sources of financing in order of desirability are:

1. Your credit union, if you belong to one.
2. Your bank.
3. A loan company or a dealer. Small loan companies deal with high credit risks, so everyone who borrows from them must help pay for the defaulted loan. If you borrow through your dealer you'll probably pay two profits, one for him and one for the financing agency.

Third, highly respected agencies such as General Motors Acceptance Corporation (GMAC), Ford Motor Company, and Chrysler Financial Corporation don't follow the same interest rates from dealer to dealer. In some cases dealers try to get all the money the market will stand. Interest on used cars may run 20 to 30 percent annual rate.

I've gone into the car-buying matter rather fully because it involves a family's largest purchases, except home owner-ship. In fact, if you buy a new car every two years you will probably spend more money for them during your lifetime than you will for your home. If you trade every two years at present prices you will pay about $50,000 for cars in forty years. And you won't have a $50,000 asset to show for it. The interest alone can add up to more than $14,000.

A good rule to follow in buying cars is to make sure that every time you trade you come out with less debt than you had the last time you changed. Then work toward zero debt so you don't add the burden of interest to the cost of the car. You need a car, but you don't have to have a new one; you don't have to change every year or two. If you owe money on the one you now have, plan to drive it at least a year beyond the time it will be paid for. During that time save the amount you are paying on the one you have. You'll earn interest on what you save and be able to buy your next car with less debt. You'll begin to see how wonderful it is when interest flows toward you instead of away from you.

If you put $100 a month in a savings account at a bank or a savings and loan company you'll have the $1,200 plus $30 or more interest. That $1,230 with your present car will help you get into a good late model with reduced indebtedness. Continue that procedure and you'll eventually have a car that's all yours.

Revolving charge accounts probably enslave more people than any other form of debt. Banks, oil companies, and department stores are glad to welcome you to the magic kingdom of the plastic card—buy what you want, up to the liberal limit, and pay a little on it each month. Some supermarkets now accept bank credit cards. Families that should carefully control their expenditures are encouraged to get what they want on credit. But if they can't pay cash for groceries this week, how can they pay for them next month with the interest added on?

And the interest can really hurt. The usual rate is 1.5 percent a month, or 18 percent a year. It can legally be quoted as the true percentage rate because it is calculated on the unpaid balance. But the way it is figured makes a difference. Some charge interest on the closing balance the previous month, so you pay interest on the payments you make or the merchandise you return during the month. Others apply the interest charge to the average balance for the month. Though the official rate is 18 percent you may pay 24 percent or more.

Revolving charge accounts have a tendency to grow. Once you are locked in, it's very difficult to get loose because your money is committed to payments. As a result you may be paying 25 percent or more extra for everything you buy.

CREDIT BUYING AND STANDARD OF LIVING

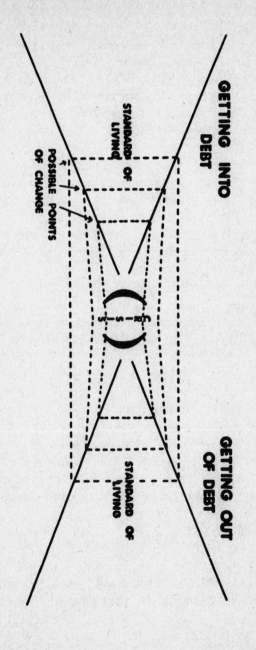

GETTING INTO DEBT

STANDARD OF LIVING

POSSIBLE POINTS OF CHANGE

CRISIS

GETTING OUT OF DEBT

STANDARD OF LIVING

The more you buy on credit
the less you can buy.

Why do you buy on credit? Perhaps because you can have what you want now, or because it seems to be the thing to do. Maybe you want a higher standard of living. But credit doesn't raise your standard of living; it lowers it.

The chart on page 63 shows how credit affects your standard of living. The more you buy on credit, the less you can buy. The credit charges eat into your income with an insatiable appetite. The credit path can bring you to crisis, from which you can escape only with great difficulty and embarrassment. And your Christian testimony may be compromised.

But, as the chart shows, you can change your course at any point. It's never too late; it's never too soon. The longer you wait the more stringently you will have to control your spending. The sooner you change the easier you'll find the recovery. Delay will hurt you.

The first thing to remember about interest is that it is the rent you pay on the money you borrow. You'll never get it back; so don't rent money unless there is no other way. And don't say there isn't any other way unless you've checked out all the possibilities you can think of.

The best plan is to pay cash. But how can you do that? It takes all you can earn to live, so how can you save enough money to buy a car or a television? But if you can't pay for it before you buy, how can you after you buy with the finance charges added on? I know you may need to finance a car, but, as I have already suggested, you should make sure you're working the balance down. And we don't have to change as often as we may think we do. Take care of it, keep it in repair, make it do.

We decided to buy a new television. Our old one, which we bought in 1960, had just about winked its last. We watched for sales and checked ratings of different makes. We bought a color set for $450, marked down from $495, and paid cash. By saving in advance it was paid for before we bought it.

But what if you want a new television and don't have the money? How do you get it? Let's start with the worst way and work up. You could get the money from a small loan finance company. But its "money rent" would be high—from 21 percent to 30 percent annual rate. On a two-year contract for $450, that would add from $95 to $135 to the cost of your TV, plus any charges for insurance and credit service.

The store would arrange financing for you. That's convenient, but it's also expensive. Stores often sell contracts to finance companies that have no concern about the performance of the product. The interest may run as high as dealing with the small loan companies. Large stores usually handle their financing and charge about 1.5 percent per month. That will run from 18 percent to 24 percent per year depending on how the interest is calculated. It would cost you an extra $81 to $108 plus miscellaneous charges. Bank credit card purchases carry similar charges.

You could deal directly with your bank. It would probably charge you about 7 to 10 percent interest, or almost 14 to 20 percent annual rate. That would cost you $63 to $90, plus any extra charges.

But there's a better way: pay for it before you buy by saving first. On the other plans you would pay from $21.38 to $23.81 per month for 24 months. If you will put $23 a month into savings, you will have $437 at the end of 19 months. It will earn about $15 interest, so your TV will only cost you $433. And it will be paid for five months sooner. If you'll continue your savings deposits to the end of 24 months, you'll have your TV, $115 saved, and $5.75 interest. Just be sure you put your money in an account that pays interest from day of deposit to day of withdrawal.

The "save first" plan will cost you at least 18 percent less than bank financing, 22 percent less than store or credit card financing, and 26 percent less than a finance company loan.

Benjamin Franklin said, "A penny saved is a penny earned." But that's not quite right. Money saved is *better* than money earned because you don't have to pay taxes on it.

In a group where my concept of zero debt was being discussed a man asked, "How long should a family plan to take to reach zero debt? Would you say ten years, to get furniture, a car, and all the things you need?"

I explained that the debt acceptance attitude always endangers family financial freedom. If we believe it is inevitable, it will be for us. If we think we can plan on a ten-year period to pay off things like furniture and appliances we will probably always be in debt. Before we pay out we will be buying more. Credit makes everything we buy cost more, so we can't have as much.

I told the group about Jim and Shirley. Soon after they were married they talked with me about their budget. Their income was quite modest. They used what money they had to buy a good bed. Friends and relatives gave or loaned them furniture. They bought a few used pieces, including a black and white television. They started a systematic savings program. They paid cash for everything, waiting till they had it to buy.

Jim and Shirley have gradually bought clothes and furniture as they have been able. They have gone into business for themselves, which required the purchase of equipment. They have money in the bank. Their apartment doesn't look as plush as some, but they have financial freedom.

CHAPTER 8

WHY SAVE?

Maybe you've gotten the idea by now that I think you ought to save. You're right. Some of every dollar you earn is yours to keep. But you'll never save it unless you pay yourself first. After your tithe and gifts to the Lord's work, your savings program should have top priority.

"We can't save now. We've got too many bills to pay. It takes everything we make just to keep our heads above water." I've heard that over and over as I've worked with couples. But unless they learn that responsible money management must include savings they may never get their debts paid. Does that sound strange? Let me tell you why it isn't.

Christian money management demands responsibility. That includes both the support of the church and the payment of our bills. You don't wait to tithe till your debts are paid, for you owe God something. It represents our acknowledgment of God's ownership. We belong to him. All we have, we receive from him. When we give one-tenth to him, he gives us the privilege of managing the nine-tenths for him. Tithing and good money management reinforce each other. And God adds his miracles to our faithfulness.

But what has that to do with savings? The principle is the same. Sound family money management must have the foundation of our own money. If you are in financial difficulty it may stem from your inability to operate on your own capital. You use credit too freely and it erodes your earnings. You must build a financial base through savings that will give you independence in how you spend what you make. You must have money that will work for you.

Your responsibilities to your church, your family, your creditors, and others will find their fulfillment in your total financial management. That will include tithing, saving, paying your bills, and planning for the future. In chapter 6 I explained how you can use the 10–70–20 plan to bring your family to the place of full fiscal responsibility. You need to work all phases of the plan at the same time.

"But what should we save for?" he asked.

"Why, to buy what we need, of course," she said.

I'm afraid they both missed the point. He had no concept of long-range saving of money to work for them. She was thinking of a spending plan, not a saving plan.

But it is a good question—just about every couple I talk with asks it. Most of them are oriented more to spending than to saving. When I tell them where to start they usually think it's an impossible dream.

You should begin your savings plan by building a buffer fund that will protect you against emergencies. How much should it be? Most financial advisers suggest six months of your take-home pay. You need that to protect you from disability, unemployment, and unexpected major problems. If you net $600 a month you should have a buffer fund of $3,600; if it's $800 you need $4,800 in reserve. Where both husband and wife work your fund should equal six months' take-home pay for the two. When you start building your basic financial reserve you'll be on your way to financial freedom.

Does that sound impossible? It really isn't. If you work the 10–70–20 plan, the 10 percent can build your fund while you live on the 70 and pay off your bills with the 20. Even if you have to put less in your savings till you get some of your debts paid you'll be moving in the right direction. When they are paid the 20 percent can go to the buffer reserve till you reach your goal. Then you'll move on to a strong saving and investment program that will give you security for the future.

When we started our zero debt program we committed a certain amount to regular long-term savings. We made sure we put that away every payday. Then we saved everything else we could. We've been surprised how well it has worked. Your buffer fund should be kept quite liquid, so you can get at it when you need it. But it shouldn't be used to buy Jimmy a pair of shoes or dad a new bowling ball. You must handle it as an emergency reserve, not a fund to take care of your wants or even needs. If you lose your job, if you have burdensome medical expenses, or if tragedy breaks in on you it will help bring you through.

Some of your buffer fund should be kept in a passbook savings account; most of it can be kept in a one-year time deposit. It will earn more interest and you can borrow against it if you have to have it before it matures.

When your buffer fund is firmly established you can use some of it to finance major purchases, if you do it carefully. For example, if you must buy a car and need $2,000 to pay for it you may do well to loan the money to yourself. But you should set some limits. Don't loan yourself more than half the fund, and don't make more than one loan at a time. Use it only for major purchases that will continue to have value against which you could borrow money if you need to. You should have no other loan on what you are financing. And set up a firm program to repay it. If you are buying a car the transportation item of your budget should carry an allowance to take care of the loan in not more than two years. When you make the purchase you can show the amount used as an expenditure and carry the negative balance forward from month to month. Make sure it's coming down all the time.

All it will cost you to finance your car that way will be the interest you won't get. And by keeping the car free and clear you can borrow on it if catastrophe hits you.

One day when I was explaining this to a group a man said, "But even if I have the money isn't it about as cheap to borrow for the car? My money will keep on earning and I'll get some tax deduction for the interest I pay. Besides, I get insurance with the loan so the car would be paid off if I should die."

Let's dispose of the insurance matter first. There are two answers that are better than insurance with financing. The best is to have a total insurance program that protects your family. The other is to buy term insurance for any special needs. You don't get insurance free with a loan. What you spend for it will do you more good in a balanced program.

Now let's consider the relative cost of using your own

money or getting a loan. The inquirer's assumption, which he got from an automobile dealer, missed two main facts about interest. First, add-on interest of 6 percent, which he quoted, amounts to almost 12 percent annual rate. Second, when you borrow your own funds and pay them back on a regular schedule you lose interest on only half of the "self loan." On add-on interest you pay the full rate for the entire period.

I took $4,000 for an example and calculated it both ways. Here's what it looks like:

$4,000 Financed

BANK LOAN	$720.00	
6 percent add-on interest		
36 payments $131.11		
Less 20 percent tax credit	144.00	
Net cost		$576.00
OWN SAVINGS	$305.91	
5.25 percent simple interest		
33 payments $130.48		
Less 20 percent tax on		
interest not earned	61.18	
Net cost		$244.13
Saving of own funds over bank loan		$331.87
Net saving of 57.6 percent		

Your savings would be replenished in 33 months by payments approximately the same as the 36 bank loan payments. If you continue monthly deposits to the end of 36 months, you will have $391.44, plus $2.57 interest for a total of $394.01.

Add to that the $331.87 you save in interest, and you will be on your way toward paying for your next car.

You'll want to make sure your debts are coming down and your savings are going up. Begin to go beyond your buffer fund with long-term savings. That's money you will put to work for you. You shouldn't plan to ever spend it. Let it grow and it will help you have a good income in retirement and provide for your family and for Christian work after you are gone. George Bowman's *How to Succeed with Your Money* will give you more help here.

You will want to save for retirement. If you work for a company that has a pension plan, check on the possibility of adding to the amount you are required to put in. Some plans provide good returns. If you are not under a pension plan you should check out the possibility of a private plan. A percentage of your income may be exempt from tax if you put it into an approved company or private pension. You'll pay tax on it when you receive it after retirement. But then you'll have a double exemption and any income you have from Social Security will be tax free. The Commerce Clearing House, Inc., 4025 West Peterson Avenue, Chicago, Illinois, 60646 has published *New 1974 Tax-Saving Plans for Self-Employed*. You may secure it for $1.50. For details on specific self-employment retirement plans you can check with savings institutions, banks, and insurance companies.

Do you ever save to spend? Yes, of course. But don't confuse that with saving to save. Keep your saving plan clear; then set your goals and lay your plans for what you want to do.

If you have children, their education should be one of your main goals. Whether they go to college or a technical school you need to be prepared. Don't wait till they are high school seniors to start saving. The sooner you begin the more interest the money you save will earn. Some plan for their children's education through insurance. If you do that, don't put the insurance on the children, but on the breadwinner. You'll probably do better to buy term insurance for protection and save at a savings and loan or a bank. If you belong to a credit union it will pay the most interest.

Christian parents need to watch their values when it's time for their children to pick a college. You may be tempted to let them go to a college or university without Christian commitment because of cost. But if you want them to get an education that is academically sound and Christ-centered, help them choose a good Christian college. It will be worth every penny it costs you.

When the children are through college and on their own you'll want some money to do some things you've dreamed about. Good money management doesn't destroy your dreams; it helps them come true. Dreaming, planning, and saving go together. They keep each other in balance. So don't be afraid to dream and plan and save. You'll find your dreams won't just be fulfilled; they'll be superseded.

CHAPTER 9

BUY RIGHT

Good money management requires careful buying. To put money into savings and pay off your bills you need to get the most you can for every dollar you spend.

That doesn't mean you always buy the cheapest thing you can get. Cheap goods can be expensive. If shoes don't last and if they hurt your feet any price is too much. If canned green beans are so woody you can't chew them, they are expensive no matter what you pay for them. On the other hand, the most expensive is not always the best buy. You usually do well to follow the medium range, but every purchase should be made thoughtfully.

Good buying begins with good planning. If you've worked out your budget carefully you have taken the first step. By looking back at what you have spent you have judged what you will need. If you keep a complete spending record you can tell how it works out. That will help you adjust as necessary to keep your whole budget in balance.

When you go to the market, the department store, or the appliance dealer you should shop for value. That doesn't mean you buy what has the highest price tag, but the one that gives you the best value for what you pay. You can tell whether the store brand of canned peaches is as good a value as the nationally advertised one by trying a can. Don't worry if the slices are uneven, but compare the amount of fruit and juice. You may be able to save several cents a can on many items. If the amount of real food you get is satisfactory and if it is both edible and nutritious you've found a good buy.

You can get trapped by packaging if you're not careful. Generally you will do well to buy large sizes, but not always. Sometimes it's cheaper to buy two small boxes of cereal than one large one. I've found toothpaste and other drugstore items occasionally priced so the smaller size is cheaper. The only way to tell is to check the measure of what you buy with the price. If an 11-ounce box of cereal costs 69 cents and a 6-ounce box costs 49 cents the larger one is the better buy. You'll pay about 6.3 cents an ounce for it and about 7.5 cents an ounce for the smaller one. But what if the small one is 35 cents? The small size is cheaper per ounce. It will pay you to have a note pad with you when you shop. Take time to divide the price by the weight. You'll save money.

Some find that powdered skim milk can save them money. Check it out and see how it compares with what you're using. You can develop a taste for it, and you can mix it with whole milk if you like it better that way. Home gardens are a popular way to save on food costs. A little experimenting will help you decide what is the best deal for your family.

Plan your meals to take advantage of seasonal prices. *Changing Times,* the Kiplinger magazine, will keep you informed on food price trends and other values. You'll find it listed under "More Helps for You," at the back of the book.

Maybe you think I'm playing with pennies. Well, I am; but pennies make dollars. They add up faster than many people think. For example, gasoline at the major stations in our area costs about 59.9 cents a gallon. The independents sell it for 53.9 to 54.9 cents. When we buy it for 53.9 cents we save six cents a gallon. That's almost 11 percent less than the major station prices. Apply that to how much gas you use in a year and you'll see it's significant. If you watch the percentages of saving on everything you buy, you can reduce your cost of living by 5 percent to 10 percent. That's like getting a raise in pay, though even better. You don't have to pay taxes on the money you save.

When you are buying according to plan you can watch for sales. But be careful, for some are real and some are phony. If an ad says "Compare with others at twice the price" it probably means the sale is not a genuine reduction. If it advertises a "special purchase of expensive suits" it's simply saying they got a good buy. You can't count on it being passed along to you.

But stores do have real sales. Supermarkets advertise "loss leaders" to get you to come in. Their weekly ads will tell you what's the best deal, usually with coupons for the bargains. You'll have to decide how much running around you can afford to do, but if you have the time and don't spend too much for gasoline, you can make money at it.

Department store sales are often seasonal. We've had January White Sales for a long time. Furniture is offered at reduced prices in August. Clothes are usually put on sale after their season. Sewing for the family brings savings and offers a sense of accomplishment. We've bought seconds on name brand clothing and found them satisfactory.

Near where we lived at one time we found an outlet store for men's clothing and a dress factory where we could buy clothes at substantial discounts. We bought good quality merchandise at discounts of 40 to 60 percent. Most major cities and some smaller ones have outlet stores. You can get some real bargains, but you need to watch for quality. Look at some good stores first, but don't buy. Then shop the outlets. Compare carefully, and you'll come out ahead.

When you look for bargains remember that it's not a bargain at all if you don't need it. Make your buying fit your plans and save you money. Then when you find what you need at the right price you can get it.

Modern merchandising is planned to make you want to buy. You start down the aisle of a store and you are cut off by a display. You can't get past it without seeing a lot of lovely items pleading for attention. Merchandising executives, psychologists, and artists have conspired to get you to buy on impulse, before you have time to think it over.

How do you avoid such a trap? First, recognize it as a trap. Second, admit that you are vulnerable. You like nice things, so it's easy for you to be tricked into impulse buying. Third, remember your spending plan. It involves the whole family. You won't spend what doesn't fit the plan because it would be unfair to the rest of the family. Fourth, limit your impulse buying to your own personal allowance money. That won't hurt anybody but yourself. After you go for broke a time or two you may be more cautious.

Watch out for emotional buying. After-argument flowers and candy often are worth the cost if they are accompanied by sharing of blame and reconciliation. However, emotional spending doesn't stop there. As a substitute for open communication it can become destructive. It's especially dangerous if it replaces the sharing of ourselves fully with our spouses or our children. Less giving of things and more giving of ourselves can bring healing to homes that are being destroyed by selfishness and materialism.

Buy right. It's a part of your stewardship. "So, whether you eat or drink, or whatever you do, do all to the glory of God" (1 Cor. 10:31).

CHAPTER 10

MAKING IT WORK

One last thing I must tell you about your financial plan: It won't work. *You* will have to work *it*.

All of your analysis and planning will be worth nothing if you don't follow through. It will take time and energy to watch your spending, monitor your savings, and keep your records. But you'll make good wages for every hour you put in. Your financial freedom will be an abundant reward for all your effort. I want to leave you with some guidelines to help you on your way.

PUT GOD FIRST

Every aspect of the Christian's life must relate to the lordship of Christ. You may be tempted to neglect your support of God's work because you have a heavy financial load. Remember these two promises of Jesus: "Seek first his kingdom and his righteousness, and all these things shall be yours as well" (Matt. 6:33) and "Give, and it will be given to you; good measure, pressed down, shaken together, running over, will be put into your lap. For the measure you give will be the measure you get back" (Luke 6:38). Practice that kind of openhandedness with God in every area of your life. You'll never be sorry.

HOLD TO YOUR PURPOSE

Your life purpose helps you go through all kinds of experiences without losing your sense of direction. Be a purposeful Christian; know why you are here and what you want to do. Keep your eyes on your financial purpose. Review it occasionally. Update it if you need to, but don't whittle away at it. It should be firm, continuing and challenging.

MOVE TOWARD YOUR GOALS

Goals should make a straight line from your purpose to your point of transfer from this life to the next. They will involve many things, but they should never draw you from your course. The reason for a goal is to help you fulfill your purpose.

Goals will change. You set them, reach them, and go beyond them. Never let yourself come to the place where you have no goal. Before you reach one, set another.

Goals are essential for a happy and fruitful retirement. They make the difference between dullness and joy. They will help you prepare financially, psychologically, and spiritually for the golden years.

KEEP COMPLETE RECORDS

There's no substitute for good financial records. With them you can tell where you are and what progress you are making. Without them you're like a ship without a chart or a compass. You're just drifting.

In addition to the basic records described earlier, you'll want to keep a file of important information. It need not be complicated. A simple box file for 8½x11-inch folders that can be found in variety stores will do. You'll need a few file folders.

Tax records are important. At the beginning of the year I set up a folder labeled "1976 Income and Deductions." Into it I put our paycheck stubs, interest payment notices, contribution records, and everything else that relates to our income and tax deductions. When it's time to prepare our tax return it's all there. After the return is finished the folder is a permanent record, which we keep. We have folders with purchases and service records of our washing machine, dryer, TV, stereo, adding machine, cars, and furniture.

INVOLVE THE WHOLE FAMILY

The family approach to financial management should not end when the budget is set up. Husband and wife should share in paying bills and keeping records. Children should participate as they are able. As soon as possible they should know what the family gives for Christian work. Their suggestions about planning and spending should be welcomed.

Total involvement in family finance helps keep the lines of communication open. Young children can't handle some information nor make major decisions. They can know they are a part of the family by being included at levels where they can participate.

Mother and father will want to discuss some matters between themselves. But they should communicate their decisions and give logical reasons. Except for these few restrictions there should be no secrets.

PLAN FOR THE UNEXPECTED

One thing you can say about the unexpected: it will come when you least expect it. Then how do you plan for it?

First, by recognizing that things do happen, both good and bad, that we haven't planned on. We have no trouble handling the good ones. But just to know that surprises will come helps us deal with them without panic.

Second, turn to God at once for his help. Don't try to go it alone. Whether the crisis is emotional, financial, or spiritual he is our greatest source of strength and direction.

Third, keep strength in reserve. Live close to God, feed on his Word, talk with him every day. Build a financial reserve. That's why you have a buffer fund. The future still belongs to those who prepare for it. Be prepared.

PROTECT YOUR CREDIT

Like fire, credit is a good servant, but a cruel master. Although I believe your goal should be zero debt, I know you sometimes need credit. It's important for you to have a good credit rating and to keep it that way. If you have a bad record you can improve it by being prompt with your payment. It will take time but you'll eventually make it.

Young people often find *good* credit hard to get. The big interest, small loan companies may let them have money, but that's expensive. There's a better way.

You can establish yourself as a good credit risk by the use of convenience credit. By that I mean you use a charge account as a convenience rather than as a method of financing. You don't put anything on the account but what you are sure you can pay when the bill comes.

For years we have charged our medical purchases. We do it

primarily to have a good record for tax purposes. We could write a check for every purchase, but it's much more convenient to write one check a month, and we have the complete record with the pharmacy.

You can handle two or three reasonable convenience credit accounts. You shouldn't have any more until you are well established. And you should pay up every one of them every month.

Occasionally you may borrow from your credit union or bank for a major purchase. Follow the guidelines I've given you. Make all payments on time.

If you now have installment payments you should pay them when due. If you can't, go talk with the creditor about it. If it's a chronic problem you need to work it out through the 10–70–20 plan.

The worst problem with credit is that it's sometimes too easy to get. It's also expensive and hard to get rid of. Use it sparingly.

Know Your Banker

Your banker can often be your best friend. He's in the money business. His success depends on the success of his depositors, so he wants to help you. Get to know him. Ask his advice. You'll be glad you did, and so will he.

Live with a Possibility Attitude

Paul wrote to the church at Philippi: "Whatever is true, whatever is honorable, whatever is just, whatever is pure, whatever is lovely, whatever is gracious, if there is any excellence, if there is anything worthy of praise, think about these things" (Phil. 4:8).

Does that describe you? Or are you culture-conditioned to react negatively, to disparage, and to discourage? Do you see problems as stoppers or as starters?

When you approach problems as opportunities your whole

outlook on life changes. In 1 Corinthians 16 Paul tells the
Christians at Corinth he plans to stay at Ephesus until Pente-
cost. He says, "For a wide door for effective work has opened
to me, and there are many adversaries." Notice he did not
say, "*But* there are many adversaries." He said, "*And* there
are many adversaries." It was not his policy to *leave* a place
because of problems, but to *stay* because of them. We need
to stay with our problems until we find the opportunities they
offer. Then, work out the solutions, and that's success.

You can't really see a problem as you ought with just a
glance over your shoulder. You need to stop, turn around,
and look it straight in the face. Walk around it. Look at it
from all angles. Try to see it from the viewpoints of other
people. Ask yourself, "What is the essence of this problem?"
But don't oversimplify it. A complex problem needs to be
divided into bite-size portions. Hack away at it until it is
broken up into component parts. Then analyze each of them.
If you do that with a positive attitude you'll find opportunities
bursting forth. Take advantage of those opportunities and
you'll be on your way.

EXTEND YOUR STEWARDSHIP BEYOND YOUR LIFE

What kind of a steward are you?

The casual steward drops a little in the offering plate now
and then, but doesn't want to be tied down to anything. The
hopeful steward gives regularly but not largely and hopes
that along with what others do it will be enough to keep the
church going. The one-tenth steward gives a tithe to God
and keeps everything else for himself. The ten-tenth steward
knows that all he has belongs to God. He not only tithes and
gives offerings, he manages money for God.

Then there is the time and eternity steward. He manages
money for God, too, but he makes sure his stewardship out-
lives him. He carefully plans so his family is cared for after

he is gone. He arranges for the distribution of part of his estate to the work of God. That's called "planned giving."

The place to start is with a will. Not a handwritten one, but a legal one, prepared by a competent attorney. Parents of minor children should be sure they have wills that specify who will raise their children in case they should both die in a common disaster. Otherwise the courts will decide.

Christian colleges, social agencies, and denominations often have expert planned-giving counselors who can advise you. Such a person can help you prepare the information you will need to give your attorney so he can draw a will to your satisfaction.

ALWAYS HAVE A DREAM

Kipling said, "If you can dream and not make dreams your master . . ." That's the way to have great joys of expectation and realization. Always live with a dream in your heart, but keep your eyes wide open.

I'm writing this on United Airlines flight 194 from Honolulu to Los Angeles on November 22. If anyone had told us in 1970 that we would vacation in Hawaii we wouldn't have believed it. On this date that year I went home from the hospital to have Thanksgiving with my family. The tests had confirmed that I had a brain tumor. After Thanksgiving I returned to the hospital for surgery on December 2.

But here we are, 37,000 feet in the air on a Boeing 747 wearing matching Aloha shirts. We've had a week of relaxation and enjoyment. We're taking home with us memories we will cherish the rest of our lives.

Why did we spend the money for the trip? Mostly because we don't want to wait too long to do some of the things we've dreamed about and saved for. My health experience impressed the uncertainty of the future upon us. We've got a good retirement program, but we want to enjoy some of the benefits of our savings now.

While in Honolulu we took a bus tour of the city. As we passed through Chinatown the driver called our attention to the Char Tour and Travel Service office, where his mother worked. We waved at her and she waved back. Then we noticed on the window the slogan, SEE THE WORLD BEFORE YOU LEAVE IT. Good financial management can help you do that, if that's what you want.

MORE HELPS FOR YOU

The more you get seriously involved in the careful management of your financial affairs the more alert you will become to other helps available. You may not want to be a financial wizard, but you can benefit from the advice of others.

The financial section of newspapers often carries columns by writers such as Sylvia Porter and Martha Patton. Popular magazines run feature articles on money management. Several magazines specialize in personal financial information. Probably the most helpful is *Changing Times,* The Kiplinger Magazine, 1729 H Street, N.W., Washington, D.C. 20006. It's well worth the subscription price of $7 per year, but you probably can get in on one of their special offers at a reduced rate.

Consumer Reports, published monthly by Consumers Union, gives much helpful product information. It has a tendency to analyze everything so much that you may wonder if anything is good, but it does make valuable comparisons. You will find it at your public library if you don't want to subscribe. If you want your own copy the address is P.O. Box 1000, Orangeburg, New York 10962. The price is $11 for one year, $20 for two years.

I recommend three books which I believe will help you:

1. Werning, Waldo, *Where Does the Money Go?* Light and Life Press, Winona Lake, Indiana 46590, 1972, $1.50.

    This is one of the best books available on the Christian philosophy of money and its management. Dr. Werning's treatment of children's growth in stewardship is especially helpful.

2. Bowman, George, *How to Succeed with Your Money*, Moody Press, Chicago, Illinois 60610, 1974, $1.25. Written by an experienced Canadian investment counselor, this book gives valuable advice about long-range financial planning. His 10–70–20 plan, to which I have referred, offers a practical way to save, live, and get out of debt.

3. Olford, Stephen, *The Grace of Giving*, Zondervan Publishing House, Grand Rapids, Michigan, 1972, $1.50. Dr. Olford deals with total commitment as the starting point of stewardship. You will find this especially helpful in establishing the spiritual basis for your financial plans.

You may find books on bargain buying on the newsstand. Some are regional and some national. *The Bargain Hunters Field Guide*, by Judith A. Bonnesen and Janet L. Burkley, lists many, but not all, outlet stores nationwide. If you don't find it locally you can get it by sending $1.50 plus 15¢ for postage to the publisher, Belmont Tower Books, 185 Madison Avenue, New York, New York 10016.

YOUR CHECKBOOK

Unfortunately, some people don't have checking accounts. They cash their paychecks, pay out for their needs, and buy money orders for payments that have to be mailed. That's both cumbersome and costly. And the presence of cash doesn't encourage thrift.

You should have a checking account into which you put all your money except savings and your current expenditures. All contributions and payments should be made by check. It's the best and easiest way to have a good record. Banks usually have several kinds of checking accounts available. Find out which one best suits your needs. Smaller banks usually charge less for their services.

Two types of checkbooks are available. One has a stub at the left where you keep a record of your last balance, any deposit you make, the amount of the check written, and the new balance. The more popular type has a separate check register, as shown on page 92. The balance at the top of the right column is from the previous page of the record. Checks and deposits are entered as shown. The checks are subtracted and the deposits are added. You don't have to subtract each check, especially if you write several at one time. Add up the total of the checks and subtract it from the previous balance. Keep current. You need to know how much money you have in the bank all the time. When you post your pay-outs to your record book, put a check mark in front of the figures in your checkbook.

Periodically—probably once a month—you get a bank statement showing your balance. But you still don't know how much money you have. You have to balance the bank's report with your checkbook. Some people panic at this point, but it's really not hard.

Most banks provide a form similar to the one on page 94 on the back of their statements. If your bank doesn't you can make up your own. After you enter the balance shown on the statement from the bank, you enter any deposits you've made that do not show on the statement. Then you stack your checks in numerical order. Check your last statement to see if you had any outstanding checks that still aren't in. You must continue to show them till you get them back from the bank.

Write the number of every outstanding check in the left column. Look up the check in your check register and enter the amount. When you come to the end of the checks you've

CHECK NO	DATE	CHECK ISSUED TO	AMOUNT OF CHECK		✔	DATE OF DEP.	AMOUNT DEPOSIT		BALANCE 184	51
403	8/3	Our Church - Tithe	30	00						
404	8/3	Dr. Smith - Bill	15	00						
405	8/6	City Electric Co.	23	80						
406	8/7	Al's Garage	25	32		8/7	285	00	375	39
407	8/8	Fidelity Ins. (Dad)	85	00					290	39
408	8/9	Ajax Drug Store	15	45					274	94
409	8/9	Mary's Dress Shop (Mom)	23	82						
410	8/10	Our Church - Tithe	30	00					221	12
411	8/12	Mrs. Jones (piano lesson)	20	00					201	12

received from the bank you can enter the next number with the word *on* after it. Then you just add up all the rest of the checks you have written. Deduct the total of outstanding checks from the bank statement balance plus additional deposits and you have your current balance.

You also should check the bank's record. Match the checks returned with the record of the checks charged to you and with your own check record. Place a mark in the designated column in the checkbook for each check that has cleared, and by all the items on the bank statement that the checks match. Remember to deduct the bank charges from your checkbook balance. If you find any discrepancies talk with the bank about it.

One thing more: be sure you don't write checks if you don't have money in the bank. The bank will make a service charge and it's hard on your credit.

MONTH _March_ 19____

THIS FORM IS PROVIDED TO HELP YOU BALANCE
YOUR BANK STATEMENT

CHECKS OUTSTANDING—NOT
CHARGED TO ACCOUNT

NO.	$	
404	28	40
409 on	43	38
420	12	60
425	5	73
427 on	67	50
TOTAL	$ 157	61

BANK BALANCE SHOWN
ON THIS STATEMENT $ 238.40

ADD +

DEPOSITS NOT CREDITED
IN THIS STATEMENT
(IF ANY) $ 285.00

TOTAL $ 523.40

SUBTRACT −
CHECKS OUTSTANDING $ 157.61

BALANCE $ 359.79

SHOULD AGREE WITH YOUR CHECK BOOK BALANCE AFTER DEDUCTING
SERVICE CHARGE (IF ANY) SHOWN ON THIS STATEMENT FOR PREVIOUS
MONTH.

INDEX

Index to Budget Record*

---

*Refer to chapter 6 for details on how to set up your budget record.

Item	Column
Freezer, home	11
Freight charges— enter with items received, sent	
Fuels of all kinds	9
Furniture bought, repairs and refinishing	11
Furniture polish	9
Fur storage	12
Games	17
Garden equipment	11
Gasoline and oil for car	15
Gifts to family members— enter as clothing, personal, recreation, etc.	
Gifts to friends, relatives	18
Gloves	12
Grass seed	10
Handkerchiefs	12
Hats	12
Hosiery	12
Hospital	14
Hunting equipment, license	17
Ice cream	8
Insurance—auto	15
furniture, house	5
health, accident	5
life	4
Interest on notes, mortgages	20
Jars, lids for canning	9
Kitchen equipment (movable)	11
Kitchen improvement (built-ins)	10
Labor costs—family laundry, housework	9
Landscaping grounds	10

Item	Column
Lawn mowing	9
Lectures	16
Licenses—auto (in some states put 6)	15
driving	15
fishing and hunting	17
Life insurance	4
Linens, household	11
Linoleum	11
Luggage	11 or 20
Magazines	16
Mailing packages—enter with item cost	
Materials—for family clothing	12
for slip-covers, etc.	11
Meals out	8 or 17
Medicines and medical treatment	14
Money order costs—enter with item ordered	
Mortgage	7
Movie equipment, film, other costs	17
Moving expense	9
Musical instruments	17
Music lessons	16
Newspapers	16
Nursing care	14
Oculist	14
Operations, surgical	14
Paint—for furniture	11
for house	10
Patterns	12
Pets, pet food and equipment	17